WHAT HAPPENS IN THE AUTUMN

by Suzanne Venino

A smiling scarecrow guards pumpkins and corn on a farm.

BOOKS FOR YOUNG EXPLORERS
NATIONAL GEOGRAPHIC SOCIETY

COPYRIGHT © 1982 NATIONAL GEOGRAPHIC SOCIETY   LIBRARY OF CONGRESS ℂIP DATA: P. 32

*A*utumn has come
to this forest. Autumn is
the season of the year when
the leaves of many trees
change color—from green
to orange, red, or yellow.
Two friends named Portia
and Shane look closely
at the bright orange leaves
of a wild cherry tree.

3

The setting sun shines
through trees in the woods.
The days grow shorter
in the autumn. Each day,
darkness comes a little bit
earlier than the day before.
But there is still enough
light for Shane to play
outside after school.

The autumn months
are September, October,
and November.
When September comes
and summer ends,
many exciting changes
take place outdoors.
You can see the changes
all around you. You can
feel them in the air.
There are cool days when
the air is clear and crisp.

Do the leaves change color in the autumn where you live? They ␣ in many places. As the leaves slowly die, the green in them disap␣

The leaves on these maple trees have turned bright colors.
Soon the leaves will come loose and drop off.

Two horses graze in a quiet pasture. There are fallen leaves on the grass. A gust of wind sends more leaves fluttering to the ground. Some leaves drop in a stream and then drift away. Soon many trees will be bare.

Fall is another name for autumn.
Do you know why? It's because this
is the season when leaves fall from trees.

*L*eaves, leaves, everywhere! Portia and Shane play in leaves they raked into a pile in Shane's backyard.

Raking leaves is an autumn chore. People often put leaves in bags to be taken away. Sometimes people put dead, rotting leaves around garden plants to help them grow.

*I*n a meadow, the children discover what happens to many plants in the autumn. They dry out, and their seeds are scattered.

The dry pods of milkweeds have burst open. The seeds inside will float away on bits of fluff like tiny parachutes. Shane blows away the seeds of a fluffy dandelion. Portia helps scatter milkweed seeds. The seeds travel far and wide. They will have room to grow into new plants in the spring.

A chipmunk has found an acorn, the fruit of an oak tree. A squirrel searches for food on the ground. In autumn, chipmunks and squirrels scurry about, gathering seeds and nuts. Chipmunks store food in their underground homes. Squirrels often bury their food. These animals may then have enough to eat in winter, when food is hard to find.

*F*all is a busy season on a farm.
It is time to harvest the crops
that have grown all summer,
and time to get ready for winter.
Portia cleans an ear of corn
she picked from a stalk.
A farmer drives a big machine
called a combine. It cuts down
the cornstalks, and it removes
the corn from the cobs.

Kernels of corn pour from
the combine into a big wagon.
During the winter, the farmer
will use the corn to feed pigs, cows,
chickens, and other farm animals.
Three pheasants search for bits
of corn left in the field.

In autumn, apples are
ripe and ready for picking.
Shane and Portia pick
apples in an orchard. Shane
bites into one right away.

Apples can be baked in pies,
pressed into cider,
or made into applesauce.
Fruit that falls to the ground
becomes food for birds,
insects, and other animals.

*I*n a pumpkin field, Portia and
Shane look for just the right pumpkin
to make into a jack-o'-lantern.
With some help from their parents,
they will hollow out the pumpkin
and carve a scary face on it.
A candle inside will shine a greeting
to children who come trick-or-treating
on Halloween night.

*L*ook up in the air! A big flock of snow geese is heading south. So are these three Canada geese. In autumn, many kinds of birds fly to warmer places where they can find food more easily.
Soon the weather will grow cold, and frost will cover the fields.

A raccoon peeks from its den in the trunk of a dead tree. The raccoon will sleep here in cold weather.

A young woodchuck spends most of the autumn eating. It eats as much food as it can find, and it grows very fat. Woodchucks sleep through most of the winter in their underground homes. In autumn, the fur of a red fox grows much thicker. The fur will keep the fox warm in the cold months ahead.

Portia and Shane run through
a clearing in the woods.
The leaves crackle and crunch
beneath their feet. What
will they find in the woods?

P ortia finds an insect called
a walking stick crawling on a leaf.
It looks like a twig with legs.

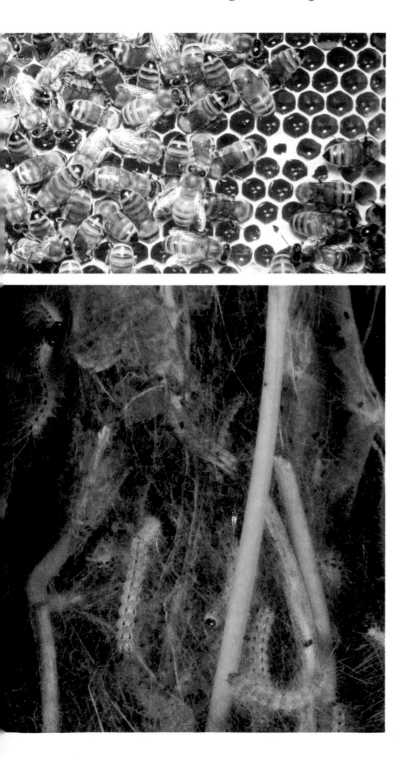

Before autumn comes, female
walking sticks lay eggs
that will hatch in the spring.
Walking sticks die in cold weather,
but some other insects do not.
In their hive, buzzing bees store
honey they will eat in winter.
Caterpillars spin a covering that
protects them. A ladybug finds
shelter under a piece of bark.

A black bear wanders around in an autumn snowstorm. In the fall, the bear looks for a den where it can spend the coldest days of winter.

Now the days are chilly. The nights are long and cold. Soon the bear will go into its cozy den and sleep. Autumn is almost over, and winter is on the way.